1/12

CR

SandCastle™

Animal Homes

# Home Sweet Den

*Mary Elizabeth Salzmann*

CONSULTING EDITOR, DIANE CRAIG, M.A./READING SPECIALIST

**ABDO**
Publishing Company

## visit us at www.abdopublishing.com

Published by ABDO Publishing Company, a division of ABDO, P.O. Box 398166, Minneapolis, Minnesota 55439. Copyright © 2012 by Abdo Consulting Group, Inc. International copyrights reserved in all countries. No part of this book may be reproduced in any form without written permission from the publisher. SandCastle™ is a trademark and logo of ABDO Publishing Company.

Printed in the United States of America, North Mankato, Minnesota
062011
092011

 PRINTED ON RECYCLED PAPER

Editor: Katherine Hengel
Content Developer: Nancy Tuminelly
Cover and Interior Design and Production: Anders Hanson, Mighty Media, Inc.
Photo Credits: Shutterstock, Peter Arnold (Klein J.-L. & Hubert M.-L, Cordier Sylvain), iStockPhoto (wayra)

Library of Congress Cataloging-in-Publication Data
Salzmann, Mary Elizabeth, 1968-
  Home sweet den / Mary Elizabeth Salzmann.
    p. cm. -- (Animal homes)
  ISBN 978-1-61714-817-0
  1. Animals--Habitations--Juvenile literature.  I. Title.
QL756.S257 2012
591.56′4--dc22

                    2010053275

---

## SANDCASTLE™ LEVEL: TRANSITIONAL

SandCastle™ books are created by a team of professional educators, reading specialists, and content developers around five essential components—phonemic awareness, phonics, vocabulary, text comprehension, and fluency—to assist young readers as they develop reading skills and strategies and increase their general knowledge. All books are written, reviewed, and leveled for guided reading, early reading intervention, and Accelerated Reader® programs for use in shared, guided, and independent reading and writing activities to support a balanced approach to literacy instruction. The SandCastle™ series has four levels that correspond to early literacy development. The levels are provided to help teachers and parents select appropriate books for young readers.

| Emerging Readers | Beginning Readers | Transitional Readers | Fluent Readers |
|---|---|---|---|
| *(no flags)* | *(1 flag)* | *(2 flags)* | *(3 flags)* |

# Contents

| | |
|---|---|
| What Is a Den? | 4 |
| Animals and Dens | 6 |
| Bobcat | 8 |
| River Otter | 10 |
| Red Fox | 12 |
| Alaska Marmot | 14 |
| Weasel | 16 |
| Spotted Hyena | 18 |
| Arctic Wolf Pup | 20 |
| Could You Live in a Den? | 22 |
| Quiz | 23 |
| Glossary | 24 |

# What Is a Den?

A den is a kind of home for a wild animal. It is a small space where the animal feels safe.

Some dens are in caves. Some are in **hollow** logs, under tree roots, or **underground**.

# Animals and Dens

A den can be used by more than one type of animal. Some animals move into dens that other animals have left. Sometimes one animal will kick another animal out of its den.

# Bobcats live in dens.

Bobcat dens are in **hollow** logs, caves, rock piles, and thick bushes. A bobcat uses more than one den.

# River otters live in dens.

River otters choose dens near lakes and rivers. An otter's den can be in a **riverbank**, log, or rock pile. There is often an underwater **entrance** to the den.

# The red fox lives in a den.

A red fox has more than one den. It has a large den for raising **young**. The red fox also has several smaller dens. It keeps extra food in the smaller dens.

# Alaska marmots live in dens.

Alaska marmots have different dens for summer and winter. Summer dens have several **entrances**. Winter dens have only one entrance. Marmots **hibernate** in their winter dens.

# Weasels live in dens.

Weasels live in **underground** dens, **hollow** logs, or rock piles. Sometimes weasels move into the dens of their **prey**.

# The spotted hyena lives in a den.

Spotted hyenas live in family groups called clans. Baby spotted hyenas are born away from the den. The mother brings the babies to the den after a few weeks.

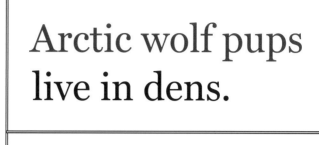

# Arctic wolf pups live in dens.

Female arctic wolves have their pups in dens. Sometimes they dig holes for dens. Or they use **hollow** logs, caves, or rock piles.

# Could *you* live in a den?

# Quiz

1. Bobcats use more than one den. *True or false?*

2. A red fox has just one den. *True or false?*

3. Alaska marmots **hibernate** in their winter dens. *True or false?*

4. Weasels never use the dens of their **prey**. *True or false?*

5. A group of spotted hyenas is called a clan. *True or false?*

# Glossary

**entrance** – a door or a way in.

**hibernate** – to pass the winter in a deep sleep.

**hollow** – having an empty space inside.

**prey** – an animal that is hunted or caught for food.

**riverbank** – land along the side of a river.

**underground** – below the surface of the earth.

**young** – an animal's babies.